Amazing Questions & Answers

Computers

Om SPARKS
An Imprint of Om Books International

Om SPARKS An Imprint of Om Books International

Reprinted in 2026

Corporate & Editorial Office
A-12, Sector 64, Noida 201 301
Uttar Pradesh, India
Phone: +91 120 477 4100
Email: editorial@ombooks.com
Website: www.ombooksinternational.com

Sales Office
107, Ansari Road, Darya Ganj
New Delhi 110 002, India
Phone: +91 11 4000 9000
Email: sales@ombooks.com
Website: www.ombooks.com

ISBN: 978-93-52766-52-9

Printed in India

10 9 8 7 6 5

What is a supercomputer?

What?

Why?

How does a computer work?

Why do we burn a CD or DVD?

How?

When?

When was the first email sent?

CONTENTS

What?

What is a computer?

A computer is an electronic device that receives information or data from us. It can store and process this information by performing calculations and operations on it. The term **computer** is derived from the Latin word '**Computare**' which means 'to compute'.

Find out

What were computers called in the 1950s?

Pocket fact

The word "computer" was first recorded in 1613. It was used to refer to a person who carried out calculations or computations.

What can we do using a computer?

A lot many things! Different people use computers for different purposes. We can use a computer to type documents, send email, play games and browse the Web. Architects, engineers, jewellers and filmmakers—all use computers to design things. Scientists, writers and teachers use computers for research. Businessmen can use computers for general record keeping. The use of computers has made many tasks easy and quick!

What makes a computer work so fast?

The processor! A computer is said to be faster and more efficient when it can carry out maximum number of instructions every second. The overall speed of a computer is managed by the Central Processing Unit (CPU). The processors today are capable of processing over 100 billion instructions per second!

Find out

When was the first supercomputer made?

Pocket fact

The Central Processing Unit is also known as the brain of the computer. It sends signals to control the other parts of the computer, almost like how the brain controls our body!

What is a supercomputer?

A very fast computer! A supercomputer has great speed and memory. It can work thousand times faster than any other computer of its generation. A supercomputer can do arithmetic calculations very fast, so it is used in advanced scientific applications, weather forecasting, and other tasks that need many calculations.

What did the first electronic computer look like?

It was the size of a room! The first electronic computer was called ENIAC- Electronic Numerical Integrator and Computer. It was built by the United States in 1945. ENIAC weighed 30 tons and used 200 kilowatts of electric power.

Pocket fact

ENIAC was no longer in use after 2 October 1955. Only about 10 panels of the 40 exist now.

Find out

Who designed the ENIAC?

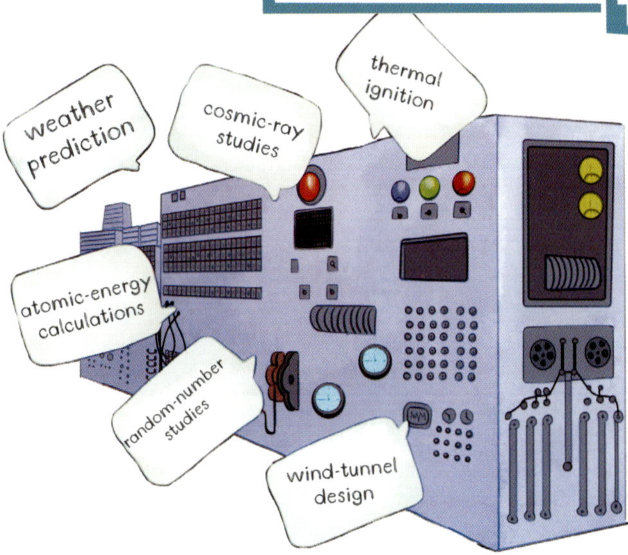

What was the first computer used for?

The uses of the first computer ENIAC included weather prediction, atomic-energy calculations, cosmic-ray studies, thermal ignition, random-number studies and wind-tunnel design. It was also used for other scientific purposes.

What are the different types of computers?

Desktops, laptops and more! Computers come in many shapes and sizes, and they perform many different functions in our daily lives. The different types of computers are *personal computer*, *workstation*, *minicomputer*, *mainframe* and *supercomputer*. Desktop, laptop, notebook and palmtop are some kinds of personal computers.

Find out

What is a stylus?

Pocket fact

The GriDPad!

The GRiDPad was one of the earliest tablets produced in 1989. It had a touch screen and a wired stylus; and weighed just under 5 pounds.

What is a tablet PC?

A Tablet PC or tablet is a small portable computer that is usually smaller than a laptop. It doesn't have a keyboard or a mouse instead has a touch-sensitive screen for typing and navigation. You can do many of the same things using a tablet like that of a desktop—browse the Internet, use apps and also display HD videos.

What is the Little Man Computer?

The Little Man Computer (LMC) is an instructional model of a computer, created by Dr. Stuart Madnick in 1965. The LMC is generally used to teach students, because it models a simple von Neumann architecture computer—which has all the basic features of a modern computer.

> **Pocket fact**
>
> In a laptop, a touch pad can be used in place of an external mouse. It helps you to move the cursor with your finger.

> **Find out**
>
> What is a computer notebook?

What was the first portable computer?

The first truly portable computer was the Osborne I developed by Adam Osborne. It was released in April 1981 by the Osborne Computer Corporation. The Osborne I was quite different from the modern laptop. It weighed 24.5 pounds and had a 5-inch display.

What is hardware?

Any part of your computer that you can see and touch! Computer hardware refers to the physical parts of a computer, such as the monitor, keyboard, mouse, speakers and CPU. It also includes all of the computer's internal parts.

Find out

Who was Ada Lovelace?

Pocket fact

Z1!

The first computer was called Z1. It was invented by Konrad Zuse in 1936. It had many parts like that of a modern computer—control unit, memory and input-output devices.

What is software?

A set of instructions that tells the computer what and how to do! Software helps us to interact with a computer, its hardware, and perform tasks. Web browsers, games, and apps are examples of software. Without software, most computers would not be able to perform.

What are the main parts of a computer?

A computer generally consists of several different parts that help it function. But the main parts of a desktop computer include the monitor, the system unit, and the keyboard. The system unit contains the hard drive, disc drive, CPU, graphics card, sound card, and many ports that connect external devices to your computer.

Find out

Which is the longest key on the keyboard?

Pocket fact

The modern computer keyboard was inspired from the invention of the typewriter in 1868. It was Christopher Latham Sholes who invented the QWERTY keyboard that we commonly use today.

What is a keyboard used for?

To communicate with the computer! The keyboard is an input device that is used to enter text. It lets us enter characters and functions into the computer by pressing buttons, or keys. Without the keyboard, it is impossible to type or enter text into the computer!

What is the number of keys on a keyboard?

It varies from one kind to another! A computer keyboard usually has 101 to 104 keys. These are Alphabet keys, Number keys, Function keys, Arrow keys, Symbol Keys and Special keys. A computer keyboard is quite similar to a typewriter.

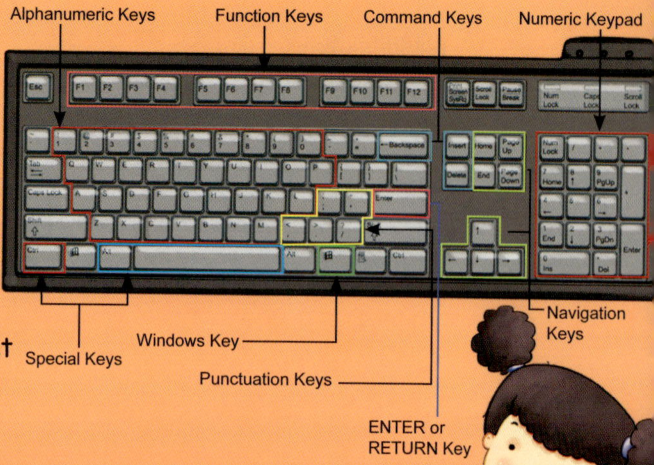

Pocket fact

The French Version!
The AZERTY Keyboard is the French version of the standard QWERTY keyboard. In such a keyboard the Q and W keys have been interchanged with the A and Z keys.

Try this

Find the keys that spell the letters of your name. In which row are they placed on the keyboard?

What is a QWERTY keyboard?

The QWERTY keyboard is the most widely used keyboard layout. It is named so because the sequence of the first six letters from the top left of the keyboard is QWERTY.

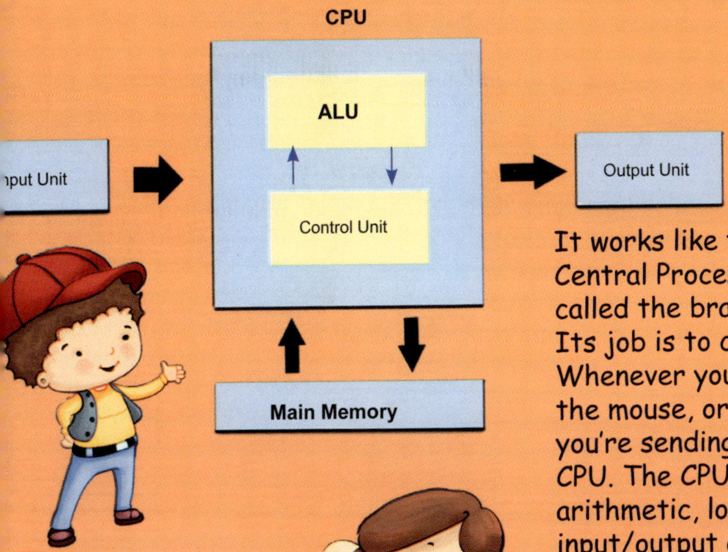

What does the CPU do for a computer?

It works like the brain! CPU i.e. the Central Processing Unit is often called the brain of the computer. Its job is to carry out commands. Whenever you press a key, click the mouse, or start an application, you're sending instructions to the CPU. The CPU then performs the arithmetic, logical, control and input/output operations specified by our instructions and gives us results.

Pocket fact

Bits and Bytes!

A bit is the smallest unit of computer's memory. A set of 8 bits is called a Byte.

Find out

What is clock rate?

What is a computer memory?

A device that stores data or instructions! A computer memory is a space inside the computer where data is stored. It is divided into a large number of small parts called cells. Each cell has a unique address, which varies from zero to memory size minus one. A computer memory is of two types—primary and secondary.

What does a computer mouse do?

It is a pointing device! A mouse is a cursor-control device that has a small palm size box with a round ball at its base. This ball senses the movement of the mouse and sends signals to the CPU when the mouse buttons are pressed. It is used to control the position of the cursor on the screen, but it cannot be used to enter text into the computer.

Try this

Can you name the parts of a computer mouse? Give it a try.

Pocket fact

The Mouse Wheel
The modern desktop computer mouse also usually includes a mouse wheel that allows you to scroll up and down on a page.

What did the first computer mouse look like?

It was much larger than today's mouse! The first computer mouse was invented by a U.S. engineer Douglas Engelbart in the early 1960s. It was made of wood, rectangular in shape, and had a small button on the top right corner. Its wooden base also had two wheels to roll back and forth.

What is a desktop?

The desktop is the area of a computer screen where we see images, windows, icons and other graphical items. Some of the most common icons on the desktop are My Computer, Recycle Bin, Internet browser and My Documents.

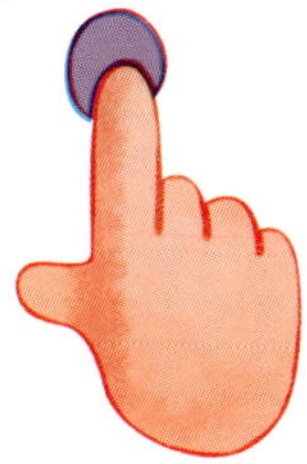

Find out

Which alphabet key should you press with the Windows key to get to the desktop?

Pocket fact

The first computer that used a monitor was the Alto. Before that computers made use of television screens as monitors.

What is the START button on the desktop used for?

To help you use programs on the computer! The Start button is found at the bottom left part of a desktop screen. When you click the Start button, the Start Menu opens and you can access all the programs installed on your computer. It acts like a window to enter your computer.

What is a USB port?

A USB port is a small port that allows different devices to be connected to a computer. Some examples of devices that connect to a USB port are printers, keyboards, computer mice, MP3 players and external hard drives. A desktop computer usually has two to four ports in the front and two to eight ports at the back.

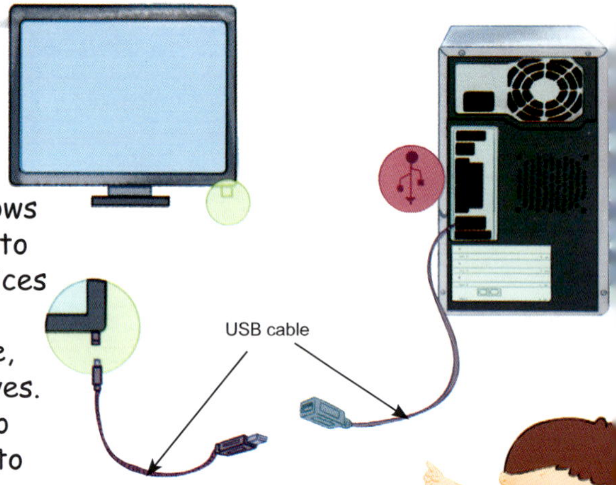

Find out

What are the other names of a pen drive?

Pocket fact

We invented it!
Pen drives were first invented at M-Systems, an Israeli company, in April 1999 by Amir Ban, Dov Moran and Oron Ogdan.

What is a pen drive?

A memory and data transfer device! A pen drive is a device used for storing and transferring audio, video and data files from one computer to another. It is often the size of our thumb and is also called a thumb drive. It connects to a computer through a USB port. Pen drives are available in sizes ranging from 2 GB to 1 TB.

What is a computer virus?

Something that makes our computer sick! A computer virus is a program or script that can cause damage to a computer by stealing information, modifying data, sending e-mail and displaying messages. When the virus is executed, it spreads in the computer by copying itself into or over the files in our computer and affects its working just like a virus makes us sick!

Pocket fact

The Creeper virus is usually recognised as the first computer virus. It was first detected on ARPANET—a network that was used before the Internet, in the early 1970s.

Find out

Which was the first antivirus program?

What can I do to protect my computer from virus?

By using an antivirus! An antivirus is a software program designed to protect your computer from computer viruses. When the antivirus detects a virus, it displays a warning asking what action should be performed. It often displays the options to remove, ignore, or move the file to the vault.

Why?

Why is starting a computer called "booting up"?

It comes from the old expression "pulling up by your bootstraps! Your computer has a lot of work to do before it is actually ready to work. When you switch on the computer, it checks the RAM as well as information about drives in your computer. A memory chip called the BIOS chip (Basic Input/ Output System) stores all of this information. Once your computer has checked to make sure everything is working, it will display the desktop screen. This process of starting up is called 'booting up'.

> **Pocket fact**
>
> **Boot Loader!**
> A boot loader is a computer program that loads an operating system or some other system software for the computer.

> **Try this**
>
> Switch on your computer and note the time it takes to boot up.

Why does my computer make funny noises when I turn it on?

It's because the hard drive has to start up! When you turn on the computer, the hard drive starts spinning the platters inside. This is what makes the whining sound that you hear at first. Then, there's a clicking sound as the hard drive moves the read/write heads back to the outer parts of the platter. These sounds are common and you usually hear them when you start your computer.

Why does a computer have a motherboard?

It is the main circuit board of the computer! The motherboard is a big board (usually green in colour) that connects all of the different parts of a computer including the CPU, memory and connectors for input and output devices. This lets all the parts of a computer work together.

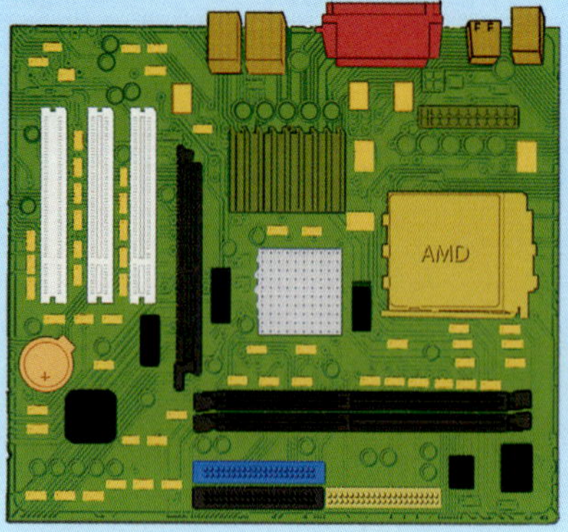

Find out

What is a daughterboard?

Pocket fact

The First Motherboard!
The first motherboard was released in 1981 and was used in the IBM Personal Computer. At that time, IBM referred to it as a "planar" instead of a motherboard.

Why are circuits in a computer so tiny?

So that the computers are of a portable size! The circuits in a computer are tiny because if the parts were larger, your computer would also be huge—maybe the size of your house and you couldn't have laptops or computer tablets! Also, the smaller you make computers, the faster they can go. By reducing the length of the wires and the distance between computer chips, you actually speed up the computer.

Why does a computer need a hard disk drive?

To permanently store and retrieve data on a computer! A hard drive is a secondary storage device that consists of one or more platters. Data is written on these platters using a magnetic head, all inside of an air-sealed casing. It is also where the computer's operating system, such as Windows or Linux is loaded.

Pocket fact

The first hard disk drive!
The first hard drive was introduced by IBM on 13 September 1956. It had a storage capacity of 5 MB and a cost of about $50,000.

Find out

What is a jump drive?

Why is the hard disk drive also called the C: drive?

Because it is the first available drive letter for hard drives! When personal computers were first invented they only had up to two floppy disk drives labelled A and B. Later, hard disks were added and were named drive C. As we install other drives, create new partitions, they will be assigned to other drive letters after C, such as D, E, F, G and so on.

Why are floppy disks called so?

They were quite fragile and tended to flop or hang loosely! A floppy or a floppy diskette is a type of storage device that can store electronic data, like a computer file. The original floppy disks were made out vinyl. These made the disks really flimsy and "floppy" hence they were named floppy disks.

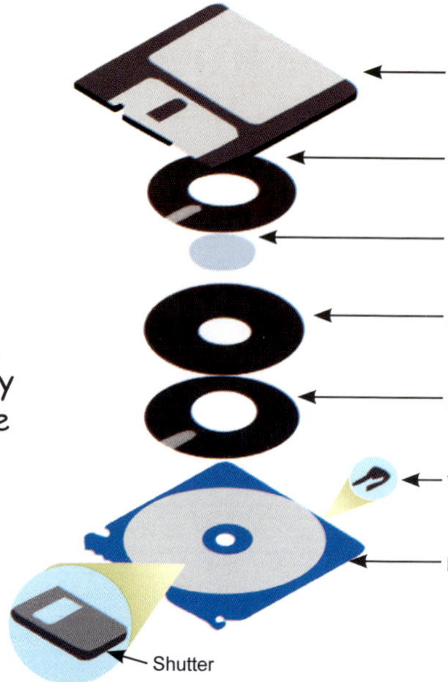

Find out

What was the size of the first floppy disks?

Pocket fact

The first floppy disk!
The first floppy disk was released in 1971. It was invented by a team of researchers at the IBM.

Pen drive

Why don't we use floppy disks anymore?

We now work with much larger files! When floppy disks were introduced, the most common format was 1.44 MB. This could hold only very small amounts of data. Computers need a floppy drive to read floppy disks and modern computers are no longer supplied with a floppy disk drive because we now work with much larger files. We can now use CDs, DVDs, pen drives and zip drives to store these files.

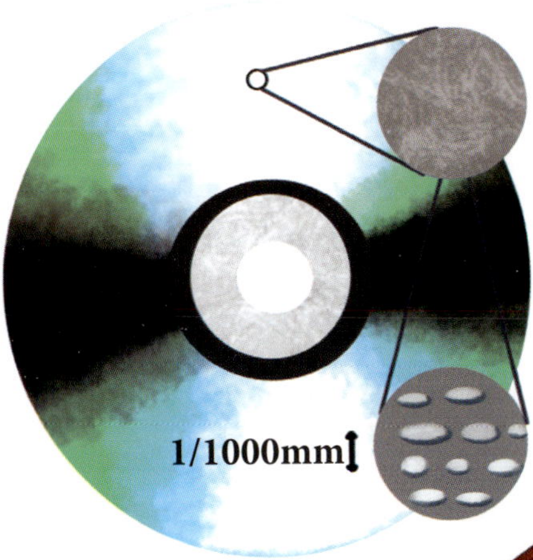

Why do CD-ROMs have little pits and scratches?

The pits are actually information! If you observe a CD-ROM with a microscope, you would see little pits and scratches on the compact disc. These pits are actually information! When the disc spins in the CD-ROM drive, a laser beam flashes on the pits and the computer reads the information off the disc.

Pocket fact

The first CD-ROM Format!
The CD-ROM format was first developed by the company Denon in 1982. It expanded on the Compact Disc Digital Audio (CDDA) format and created the CD-ROM format. This allowed it to store not only audio files but also other forms of data.

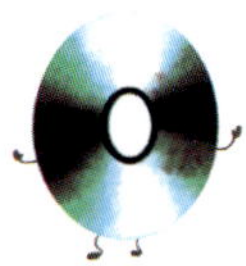

Find out

What is another name for a CD ROM Drive?

Why do we burn a CD or DVD?

Writing data to a CD or DVD is called burning it! When data is written to a CD or DVD, a laser is focussed at the surface of the disc to change the coating. This is called "burning" it. When the data is written, it is encoded in 0s and 1s. A darkened (burned) spot represents 0 and a translucent spot represents 1.

Why does a computer keyboard have function keys?

These keys act as shortcuts to certain functions! The function keys or f keys are lined along the top of the keyboard and labelled F1 through F12. These keys perform certain functions, like saving files or printing data. For example, the F1 key is often used as the default help key in many programs. The function of these keys differs according to the operating system and the software we use.

Find out

Where is the Fn key located on a laptop?

Why are there bumps on the F and J keys?

To help users correctly position their hands on the keyboard! You need to place your hands in an optimum position while typing on the computer. To help you with this, the F and J keys have bumps on them. The bump on the F key helps you place your left index finger and on the J key helps you place the right index finger!

Pocket fact

Function Keys (f) and Function (Fn) key are different!
The Function (Fn) key is found on most laptops and some computers to perform special functions, such as turning up the screen's brightness and adjusting speaker volume. It is different from the f1 to f12 keys on a computer!

Why is a computer mouse called so?

The first computer mouse was given its name by its inventor, Douglas Engelbart. He called it so because its wire looked like the tail of a mouse. Initially the mouse was named "X-Y Position Indicator for a Display System". But this name was not popular and the mouse was instead called "turtle," which eventually became "rodent," and at last was renamed as "mouse."

Find out

What is a spinning beach ball cursor?

Pocket fact

The Windows Wait Cursor!
The Windows wait cursor also called the hourglass cursor is a cursor that indicates that an application is busy performing an operation.

Why is the cursor of a mouse slightly tilted and not straight?

Due to low resolution displays! When the cursor of the mouse was invented, it was difficult for the developers to design a straight mouse arrow of small size. Also, the vertical arrow was not clearly visible to the users due to low resolution displays. So, instead of increasing the size of the pointer, it was slightly turned to 45^0 angle.

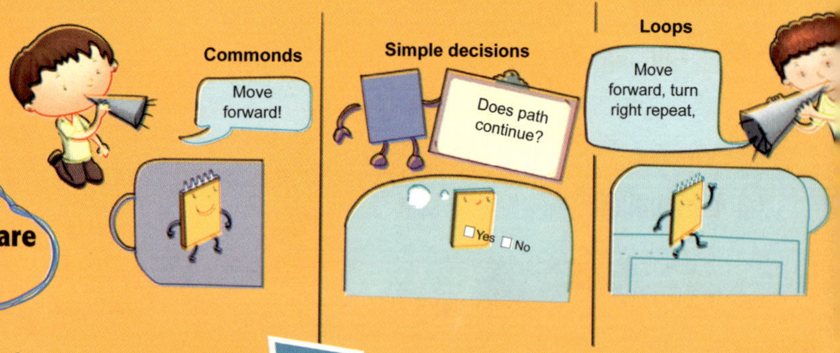

Why is software called so?

To distinguish it from hardware! Software is a program or a list of very detailed instructions telling the computer what to do. Software can be anything- from an entire operating system, such as Windows to a simple game. Hardware is something that you can touch, while software is information.

Pocket fact

Interface Manager!
The operating system Windows was first released in 1985. It was originally called Interface Manager.

Find out

What does loading software mean?

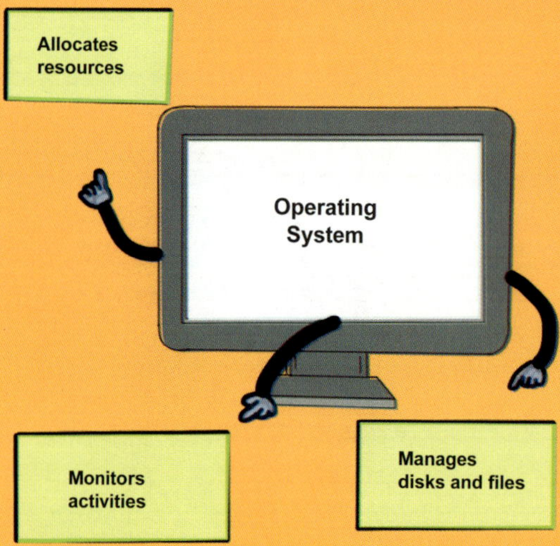

Why does a computer need an operating system?

It manages all of the software and hardware on the computer! An operating system is a software on the hard drive that enables the computer hardware to communicate and operate with the computer software. Without an operating system, a computer and software programs cannot be used.

Why does a computer need to restart after installing any software?

So that the installed software can come into effect! When a software is installed, it may require a DLL (Dynamic Link Library) file to be replaced. But it can't be done if the file is used by the operating system or any other application. So, we restart the computer after installing a software and the system is free to change the relevant files.

Pocket fact

Head Crash!
A head crash refers to the hard disk failure. It occurs when a read-write head of a hard disk drive comes in contact with its rotating platter. This results in permanent damage to the magnetic media on the platter surface.

Find out

What is a bug in computing?

Why do computers crash?

When there are bugs in the operating system! Crash is a word used to describe software and hardware failures that cause it. Sometimes when there are bugs or viruses in the software, they can cause problems with a computer's operating system. When the operating system has problems, the entire computer can freeze and crash.

Why can't a computer do without 0s and 1s?

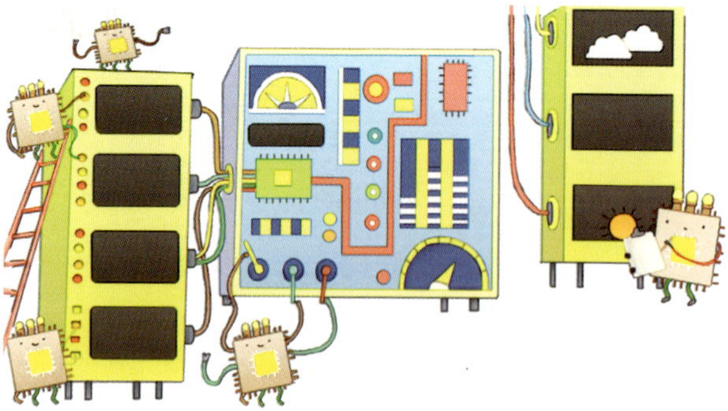

These are the only numbers a computer understands! Computers don't have brain as humans. They just understand two states- on and off, which are represented by 0 and 1. Whatever instructions we give to the computer are converted into 0 and 1. The computer processes this information and gives us the result.

Find out

What is a computer clock cycle?

Pocket fact

Either 32-bit or 64-bit!
A computer with a 32-bit processor can only have a 32-bit version of an operating system installed. It cannot have a 64-bit version of an operating system installed.

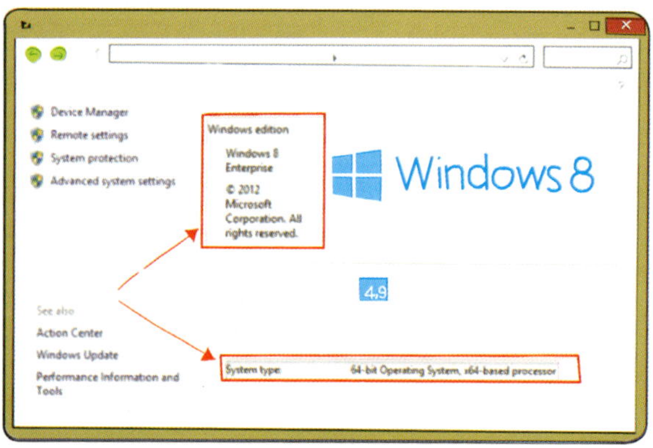

Why do computers have 32-bit and 64-bit operating systems?

It refers to the way a computer's processor, CPU handles information! 32-bit and 64-bit are types of CPU architecture that are capable of transferring bits of data per cycle. It is the amount of information your CPU can process each time it performs an operation. Computers with 64-bit operating system are faster than 32-bit operating systems.

Why do we need a modem?

To help it communicate with other computers! A modem is a device that allows your computer to communicate with other computers through a telephone line. A telephone wire is attached from the modem to a telephone jack. The modem changes your data into sounds to send it through the telephone wires, and then another modem on the other end changes the sounds back into data.

Find out

What is the full form of Modem?

Pocket fact

Dataphone!
The first Modem was known as the Dataphone. It was released by AT&T in 1960.

Why are dial-up modems so noisy?

It is the sound of your modem communicating with another modem at the other end of the phone line! Modems originally sent data over a network that was designed to only carry voice. Because of that, the communication between two modems was in the hearing range else it would not get carried on the phone line. However, modern modems are not noisy because the phone system can now carry both voice and data at the same time (DSL).

Why do different websites end in different extensions?

They help us identify different domain names on the Internet! The extensions at the end of website or domain names are called Internet domain suffixes. The **.com** tells the computer that you are looking for a commercial website. Addresses that end in **.gov** are government websites and those that end in **.edu** are colleges or universities.

Pocket fact

Scavenger hunt!

A scavenger hunt is an educational lesson which introduces the Internet to us. It is a tool that helps us follow clues to find things or guides us how to search the Internet.

Find out

What is a search engine?

Why does the Internet slow down sometimes?

There can be a number of reasons! The most common problem that slows down your Internet connection is malware, such as viruses, spyware and adware. Sometimes the fault lies with your Internet Service Provider, also known as your ISP. The ISP may experience technical difficulties from time to time. Routers and servers get overloaded and occasionally break down. When these problems arise, it often results in slow Internet connection.

Why do my parents turn on 'parental controls' on the online service?

To keep you safe on the Internet! All the online services have a feature called 'parental controls' that allows parents to keep children away from inappropriate and dangerous sites, restrict access by time. For example, no social media sites during homework time.

Pocket fact

The First Spam!

The first electronic spam mail was composed by Gary Thuerk. It was sent in 1978 as an advertising email to 393 recipients on ARPANET.

Find out

Who is a newbie?

Why shouldn't we click on unknown links in emails?

They can be malware programs! Clicking a link in an email may not always be dangerous but we should be aware of the risks. Some emails contain links to download a malicious file such as a virus Trojan or malware. Such files can harm your computer or even steal your personal information.

How?

How does a computer work?

By following the input, store, process and output cycle! The computer does its primary work in the control centre also called the CPU. When we give any instruction to the computer, it carries out our instructions and converts the input to output.

Find out

What was the Analytical Engine?

Pocket fact

Faster and Faster!
Every year computers get faster and faster, but do you know someone predicted this already? He is George Moore and his law is called Moore's Law. It says that every two years the speed of the central processor will double.

1 MHz means 1 million cycles per second

How many calculations can a computer perform per second?

It varies from one computer to another! The speed of a computer depends upon its processor. The speed at which the processor executes each instruction or each vibration of the clock is called clock speed. The processor requires a fixed number of clock ticks, or cycles, to execute each instruction. The clock speed is measured in MHz. 1 MHz means 1 million cycles per second, 1 GHz means 1 thousand million cycles per second and so on.

How many kinds of memory does a computer have?

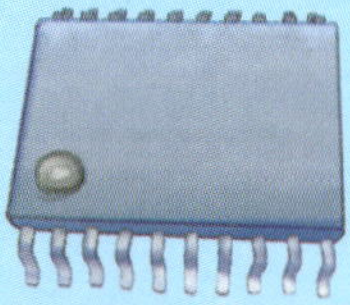

A computer has two types of memory: RAM (Random Access Memory) and ROM (Read-only Memory.) RAM is the short term memory that a computer uses for immediate tasks. It stores data and information only as long as the computer is ON. On the other hand ROM, the long term memory holds instructions and data even when the computer is OFF.

Find out

What is a hard disk?

Pocket fact

No ROM!

The earliest computers did not have ROM. When a computer was turned on, it would just do nothing until you entered the commands to start up, using a row of switches on the front of the computer. And if something went wrong, you had to start all over again!

How does a computer memory work?

Memory is the area where a computer stores data. Memory provides the CPU with its instructions. When you switch on the computer or run an application, your operating system allocates space in the RAM and makes the applications run smoothly. ROM stores important control programs and system software to perform a variety of functions, such as starting up programs.

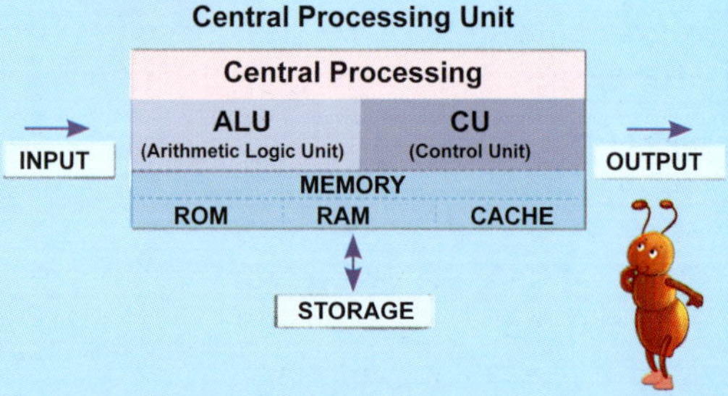

How much memory does my computer really need?

At least 32 megabytes of memory! The amount of memory that you have in your computer is very important. When we talk about memory we mean RAM (Random Access Memory). Most computers have 32 megabytes of memory installed; whereas some have 64 megabytes of memory. If a computer doesn't have enough memory, it may run very slowly or many not run some programs at all.

Pocket fact

Random Access Memory!

Computer memory is organized as a bunch of addresses, one per byte. The computer reads or writes to any address in memory without following a sequence. Hence such memory is called Random Access Memory or RAM.

Find out

Why is Read Only Memory or ROM important?

How can I add more memory to my computer?

By putting more RAM in your computer! Sometimes, your computer's hard drive makes a lot of noise and the little hard drive light on the front of your computer flashes a lot while you are using programs. This shows that you need to increase the computer's RAM. To do so, you can ask a computer store to have new RAM chips installed in your computer. This will add more memory to your computer and help it function smoothly.

How is data stored on a computer?

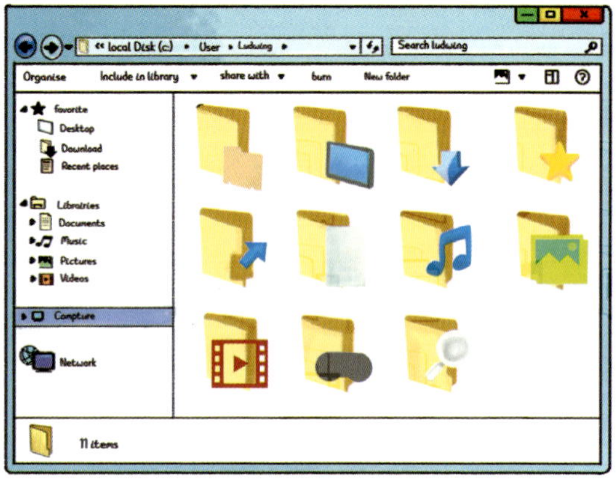

In files and folders! A computer stores a lot of data in files that are actually made up of ones and zeroes, a code that the computer understands! These numbers are called 'bits'. The different ways in which these numbers, or bits, are put together create our files. Eight bits make a bite. Thousand bites make a kilobyte. Thousand kilobytes make a megabyte and so on. Computer files are stored on a hard drive and you can use them anytime you want.

Pocket fact

Only add and subtract!

Not only can your computer count 0 and 1, it is only able to add or subtract. Even though we can do many complex calculations on a computer, deep down inside, the computer is actually only adding and subtracting 0s and 1s.

Find out

How many bytes are there in a gigabyte?

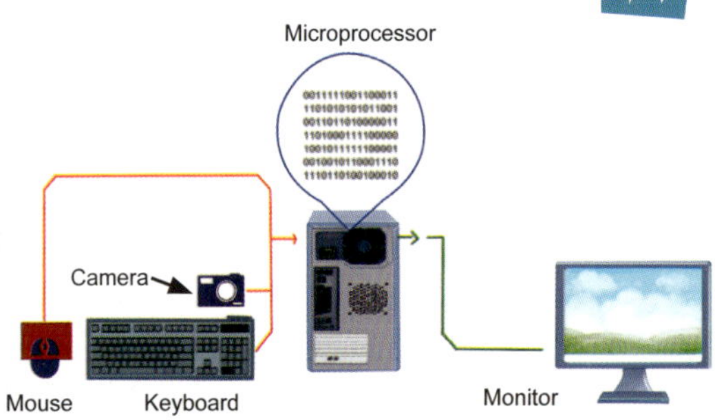

How many bits does a computer use at once?

It depends on what we ask the computer to do! A computer works in 8-bit chunks called bytes. It also works with 16 bits at a time (called a word) or 32 bits at a time (called a long word). When we work with letters, our computer moves bytes at a time. One byte stores one character like a letter, punctuation mark or space.

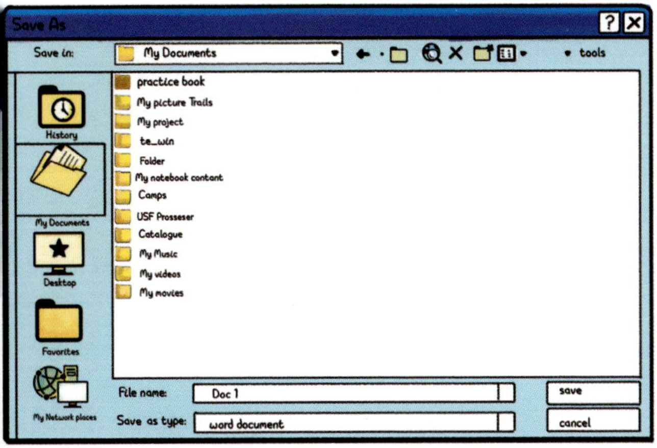

How can I save my work on a computer?

You can do lots of things on a computer. You can make a picture, write a letter or draw a chart. But it is important to save your work if you want to use it later. To save your work you need to give it a name. To do this, click the 'save' button under the file menu and store it safely on your computer.

Pocket fact

No extension!
A file in a computer has an extension. For example: a word document is saved with an extension ".doc". But a folder does not have an extension like a file.

Try it!

Create a folder on your computer desktop and give it any name you like.

How do I create folders on a computer?

We create folders for different documents, files and/or subjects to keep things organized on our computer. To do so, right click in any empty space on your computer. Then, select **New** from the list and it will expand. Select **Folder** from the new list. A new folder is created at the bottom of the list of files and folders with the name **New Folder**. It will be highlighted if you haven't moved the mouse. Type in a name for the folder, e.g. **Lessons**. Press Enter key and the folder will have the new name you typed.

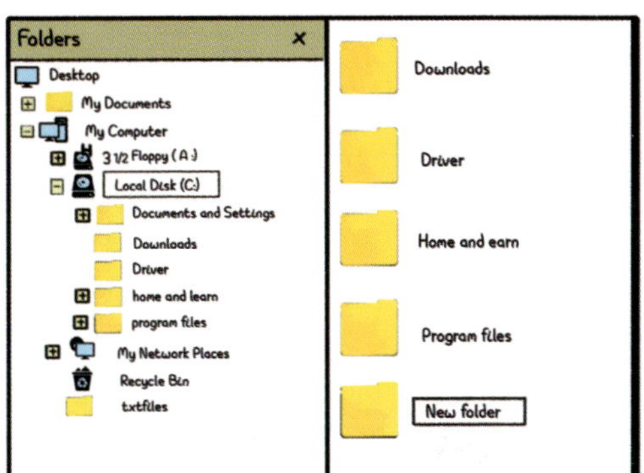

How many languages does a computer know?

Just one! Computers understand only one language which is called machine language or binary language. It is made of only two numbers—0 and 1. We give instructions to a computer in different programming languages. These are translated by the computer into binary codes before the CPU can execute them.

> **Pocket fact**
>
> **High and low-level language!**
> Computer languages are of two kinds: high-level and low-level languages. High-level languages are easier to read, write and maintain than low-level languages.

> **Find out**
>
> Do you know any computer languages? Name any two of them.

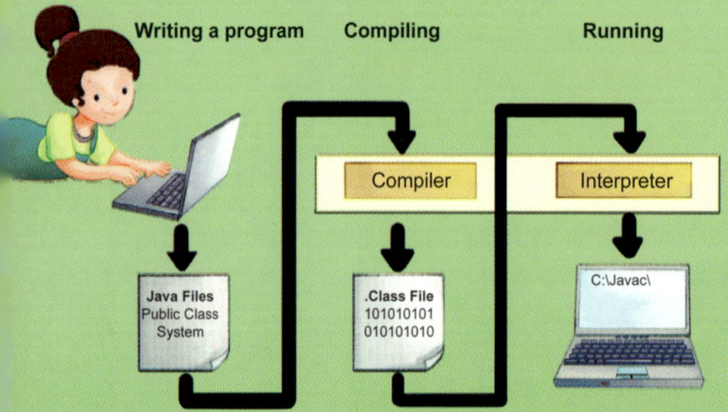

How are our instructions converted into computer language?

With the help of translators called compilers and interpreters! A computer has a piece of translator software which converts our instructions into machine code. These translators are known as compilers and interpreters. Programs are translated using either a compiler or interpreter.

How do computer keys work?

Every keyboard has a key matrix inside it. This matrix is a grid of circuits underneath the keys. When we push a key, the metal part of the circuit connects 2 wires which allow a current to flow to the computer. The computer measures the voltage and transforms the amount of volts into binary codes (0 and 1). The computer compiler reads the binary, and a letter appears on a screen.

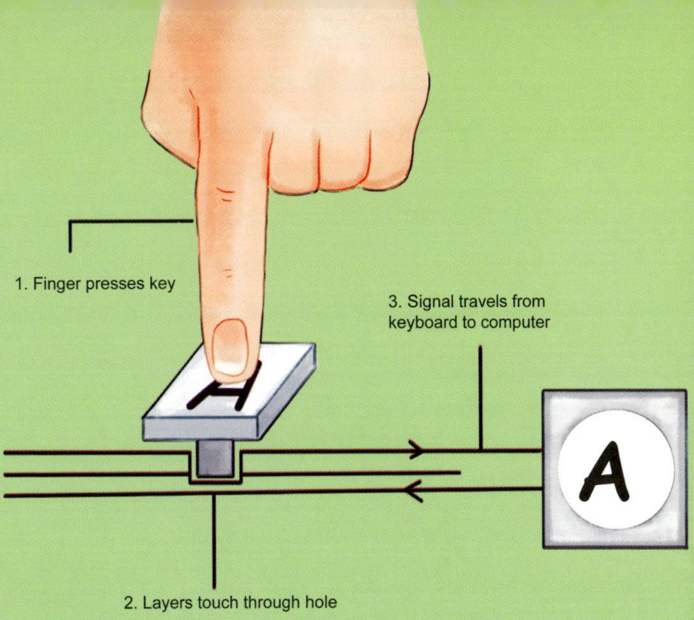

Find out

When do we use the Num lock key?

Pocket fact

Toggle key!
A toggle key is a key that is used to turn a function on or off, or to switch between two functions. Examples of toggle keys are the caps lock key, number lock key and scroll lock key.

How does a wireless keyboard work?

With the help of a battery! A wired keyboard is connected to a computer using a serial port, either by a five-pin serial connection or a USB cable. The keyboard receives power over this cable and transmits the commands to the computer. Whereas, a wireless keyboard is powered by battery and sends its signal to a receiver that is connected to the computer through a USB port.

How does a monitor work?

A cable connects the monitor to a video adaptor on the motherboard of the computer. When we work on a computer, the CPU sends instructions to the video adaptor telling what needs to be displayed on the screen. The video adaptor then converts the instructions into signals and sends it to the monitor. The monitor then generates the picture on the screen from the set of signals.

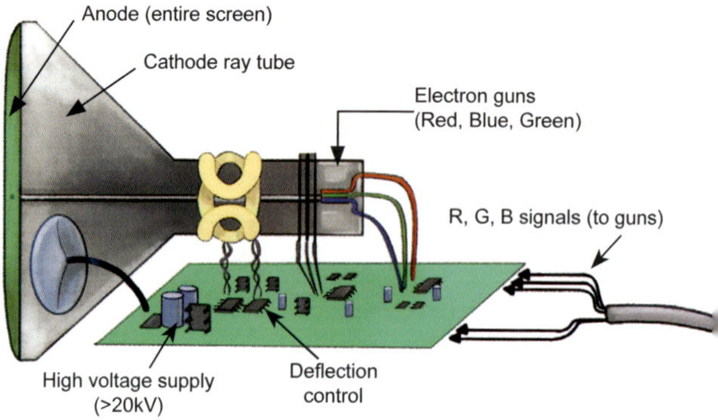

Pocket fact

The First Monitors!
The first computer monitors were modified typewriters and Teletype machines. These devices were slow, noisy and expensive, and could only handle text.

Find out

What is an MP3 file?

How can I hear sounds on my computer?

With the help of speakers and a sound card! A computer usually has speakers and a sound card (a hardware that sends sounds to the speakers) to produce sound. The sound card connects to the motherboard inside the computer. The speakers connect to the sound card through a cable at the back of the computer and help us listen to sounds.

How are hamsters and rats similar to a computer mouse?

They are actually different kinds of computer mouse! A hamster is a mouse without a cord. Most hamsters, use radio signals to transmit to the computer where the cursor is. A rat is a mouse that you move on the floor with your foot. However, computer hamsters and rats are not often used anymore because they are difficult to handle.

Find out

What is joystick?

Pocket fact

Track Point!

In some laptop computers, almost between the G and H keys, is a small rubber stick called a track point! When you move it around with your index finger, it moves the cursor.

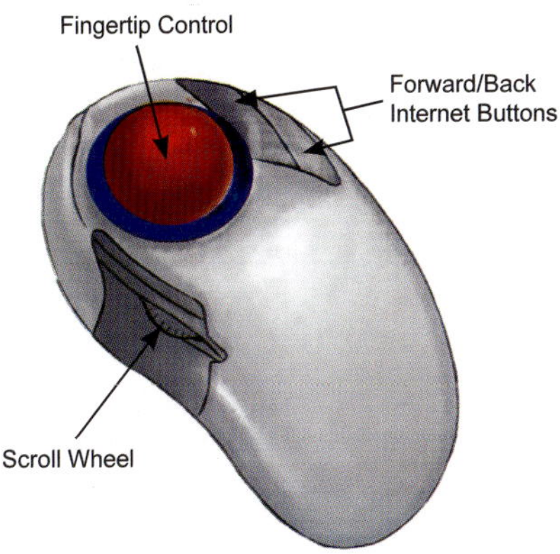

How is a trackball different from a mouse?

A trackball is a stationary pointing device with a ball on its top or side. To move the pointer using a trackball, we rotate the ball with our thumb, fingers or the palm of our hand. Whereas using a mouse, we can move the pointer on the screen to an object such as a button, a menu, an icon, a link or text. Then, we can press a mouse button to perform a certain action associated with that object.

How do computers 'talk' to each other?

By setting up network connections! Computers communicate to each other by means of network. Network connections are set up by wired or wireless means and allow computers to 'talk' to each other and share computing power. There are different kinds of network such as Personal Area Network, Local Area Network, Campus Area Network, Metropolitan Area Network, Wide Area Network, Global Area Network and Internet.

> **Pocket fact**
>
> **DARPANET!**
> In around 1960s when there was no Internet, the Department of Defense, United States created a computer network called the DARPANET. It connected the computers of the department together by a telephone wire. This led to the invention of Internet.

> **Find out**
>
> What is the difference between a web page and a website?

How do computers handshake?

By establishing rules to connect to each other! When a computer communicates with another device like a modem, printer or network server, it needs to handshake with it to establish a connection. To do so, one computer sends a message to another computer indicating that it wants to establish a communications channel. The two computers then send several messages back and forth that enable them to verify the connection, speed or the authorization of the computer trying to connect to it.

How can I make the icons on my computer easier to see?

By increasing the size of text and icons! We sometimes find the text on the screen difficult to read. To increase the size of letters and icons, go to the **Control Panel**. Under **Explore all settings**, click to select 'Make the computer easier to see'. Under **Make things on the screen larger**, press **'Alt' + 'Z'** or click to select **'Change the size of text and icons'**. You can change the text and icon size to 100% or 125% depending on your choice. Then click '**Apply**' and press '**Enter**' to accept your changes.

Pocket fact

That's an icon!
An icon (in computing) is a picture which represents a computer program, file, folder, or an action for a program to do. Icons are usually small pictures, but not always.

Try it!

Draw the icon of Recycle Bin found on your computer desktop.

How can I rotate my computer screen?

By using the Ctrl and Alt keys! Some changes in settings can cause your computer screen to turn on its side or upside down. To do so, press and hold the Ctrl and Alt keys while you press the arrow keys. Pressing these keys at the same time will rotate the screen back to the default setting.

How does a virus harm my computer?

A computer virus is a program created by someone to harm other computers. Viruses are programs that tell your computer to do something destructive. For example, if you start your word processing program, the virus might keep you from starting your computer, or it may delete all of your documents!

Find out

Which antivirus program is installed in your computer/ laptop?

Pocket fact

Do not click!
We cannot get a computer virus by just reading an email. A virus is only activated when we click a link or open an infected attachment.

How does an antivirus work?

By stopping computer viruses harm our computer! An antivirus is a program that can find viruses and stop them from doing bad things to our computer. It protects our computer by monitoring all file changes and the memory for specific virus activity patterns. When these known or suspicious patterns are detected, the antivirus warns the user about the action before they are performed.

How can you use the internet?

Computers have programs called browsers, which are used to access the World Wide Web (www). The web is one of the most important uses of the Internet. There are lots of websites on the Internet. They are made up of web pages. A web page can have videos, pictures, words and games on it.

Pocket fact

HTTP!

When you open a web page, you notice http in the address bar. HTTP refers to Hypertext Transfer Protocol. It is the set of rules for transferring files (text, graphic images, sound, video, and other multimedia files) on the World Wide Web.

Find out

Who invented the email?

How does someone shout in an email?

By writing in all capital letters! When we send an email to someone, he/she can read it but cannot actually hear your message. But an email that is typed in all capital letters, like "HI HOW ARE YOU?" is considered to be shouting! It is considered to be rude so we shouldn't write an email in all capital letters.

When?

When was the word "computer" first used?

In 1613! The word "computer" was not used for a machine but to describe a human who performed calculations or computations. The definition of a computer remained the same until the end of the 19th century, when some machines were invented whose main purpose was performing calculations.

Pocket fact

The Father of Computer!
Charles Babbage was considered the Father of Computer after the invention of the Analytical Engine.

Try this

What was the Difference Engine?

When was the first mechanical computer invented?

It was proposed in 1837! The first general mechanical computer was the Analytical Engine. Its concept was proposed by Charles Babbage in 1837. The Analytical Engine contained an Arithmetic Logic Unit (ALU), basic flow control, punch cards and integrated memory. Unfortunately, because of lack of money, Charles Babbage couldn't build this computer. In 1910, Charles Babbage's youngest son, Henry Babbage completed a portion of this machine and was able to perform basic calculations.

When was the first programmable computer made?

Between 1936 and 1938! The first programmable computer was called the Z1. It was created by a German named Konrad Zuse and is considered to be the first electro-mechanical binary programmable computer, and the first really functional modern computer.

Pocket fact

Plankalkül!
Konrad Zuse wrote the first algorithmic programming language in 1946. It was called 'Plankalkül'.

Find out

What is the full form of UNIVAC?

When was the first computer company established?

In 1948! The first computer company was the Electronic Controls Company. It was founded by J. Presper Eckert and John Mauchly who also helped to create the ENIAC computer. Later, the company was renamed as Eckert-Mauchly Computer Corporation or EMCC. It also released a series of mainframe computers under the UNIVAC name.

CBS TELEVISION
UNIVAC and the election of 1952

When did computers first appear on television?

In 1952! The first computer to appear on the television was the UNIVAC 1. It was designed by the Eckert-Mauchly Computer Corporation. UNIVAC became famous in 1952 when it was used to predict who would win the presidential election between Dwight Eisenhower and Adlai Stevenson in America. As the computer predicted, Eisenhower was the winner!

Pocket fact

The BINAC Keyboard!
The BINAC Keyboard had eight keys, representing the octal numbers zero through seven. The keys when pressed produced a unique set of binary pulse codes (3 pulse combination) to give input to the computer.

Find out

Which mathematical operations could the BINAC perform?

When was the first computer designed for an aircraft company?

In 1949! The BINAC or the Binary Automatic Computer was one of the first electronic computers. It was developed for Northrop Aircraft Company and was called the BINAC or Binary Automated Computer. The computer was able to perform high-speed arithmetic operations on binary numerals.

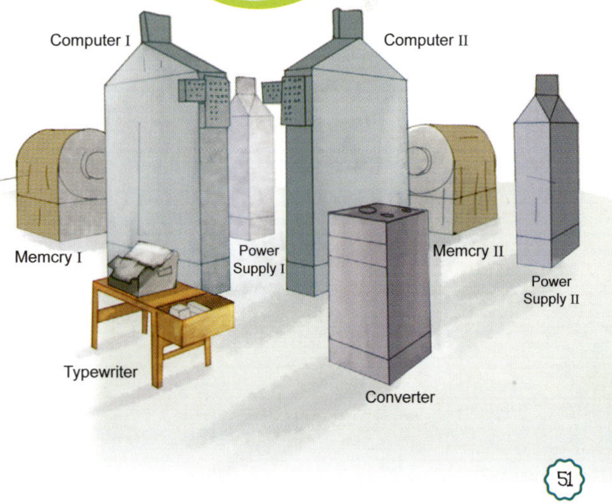

When was the first desktop computer invented?

In 1964! The first desktop computer was invented by an Italian engineer Pier Giorgio Perotto and manufactured by Olivetti. It was called the Programma 101 and was released to the public at the New York World Fair in 1964. The Programma 101 was able to perform the basic four arithmetic functions (addition, subtraction, multiplication and division), square root, absolute value, and fractional part.

Find out

When was the first personal computer invented by IBM?

Pocket fact

That's the name!

The Altair was earlier called PE-8, but Les Soloman, the writer for the Popular Electronics article wanted a catchier name. The name "Altair" was suggested by his daughter on the name of the place the Star Trek crew was travelling that week.

When was the term 'personal computer' first used?

In 1975! The term 'personal computer' was coined by Henry Edward Roberts when he introduced the computer Altair 8800. The computer had an Intel 8080 processor, "1024 word" memory boards with 256 bytes of memory (expandable to 64 KB). Interestingly, Altair did not have a keyboard, monitor, or printer and got its input from switches on the front of the computer. The switches represented either a 0 or a 1 and got output from flashing lights.

When was the first laptop invented?

In 1981! The first portable computer or laptop was developed by Adam Osborne. It was called the Osborne 1. It had 64 KB of memory, two 5 inch floppy drives and also included a modem.

Pocket fact

Dynabook!
The first idea for a tablet computer was given by American computer scientist Alan Kay in 1972. His concept was called the Dynabook. It would be a personal computing device for children that functioned similarly to a personal computer.

Find out

When was the first tablet computer invented?

When was the palmtop computer first created?

In 1989! A palmtop computer is a personal computer that is small and light enough to be held in one hand. The first palmtop computer was called the Atari Portfolio. It was released in June 1989 by the Atari Corporation. It had a very small screen but had several built-in programs like calculator, text editor, address book, clipboard and file transfer.

When could information on a floppy disk be lost?

When it is placed near a magnet! A floppy disk is a type of disk storage device made of thin and flexible magnetic disk inside a plastic case. It was widely used since 1970s until the early 2000s when new storage devices were invented. Since floppy disks store data in the form of magnetic fields, all its information can be lost if the disk is placed near a magnet.

Find out

What is the full form of USB?

Pocket fact

The Disgo!
The USB flash drive developed by the IBM was called the Disgo. It came in various sizes: 8 MB, 16 MB, 32 MB and 64 MB.

When were USB flash drives invented?

In 1998! The USB flash drive also commonly known as the pen drive is a data storage device. The first USB flash drive was invented by the company IBM in 1998. It was developed to replace the floppy drive in one of its product called ThinkPad.

When do bugs occur in a software?

When we make errors in designing a software! A software bug is an error, mistake, defect or fault, which may cause failure or deviation in a computer program. Most bugs are due to human errors in source code or its design, or by insufficient or erroneous logic while developing software.

Pocket fact

A buggy!
When a program contains a large number of bugs it is said to be buggy.

When does a computer become a zombie?

When it is hacked! A computer is called a zombie when it has been infected by a computer virus or compromised by a hacker. A zombie can be controlled under remote direction to perform unethical tasks, as well as infect other computers with viruses.

Find out

What signs show that your computer is infected with virus?

When was the first computer virus ever created?

In 1982! The first computer virus was written by Rich Skrenta in USA. The virus was called Elk Cloner. It spread to other computers by monitoring the floppy drive and copying itself to any floppy disk that was inserted into the computer. A computer infected with the Elk Corner would display a short poem on every 50th boot.

Find out

Why should we update antivirus softwares?

Pocket fact

A worm!

A computer worm is a destructive program that can replicate itself. It contains codes that help it enter computers or networks. Once within a computer or network, a worm can delete, modify, distribute and manipulate data.

When was the first antivirus program written?

In 1987! An antivirus is a program that protects your computer from virus. The first antivirus programs began to appear in 1987. It was an antivirus program from G Data Software for the Atari ST. Later in the same year, another antivirus program called VirusScan was introduced by John McAfee. Later, this came to be known as the McAfee antivirus program.

When did the Internet start?

In the late 1960s! The Internet started with the development of ARPANET that was a Wide Area Network linking many universities and research centres in the United States. It was the beginning of what we call the Internet today.

Pocket fact

Intranet!
The Intranet is a local or private network that is created using World Wide Web. It can be used only with an enterprise or organization for which it is created.

Find out

What is the difference between Internet and World Wide Web?

When was the World Wide Web introduced to people?

In 1991! The World Wide Web or WWW is a graphical interface for the Internet. It was first released on 6 August 1991 by Tim Berners Lee. The World Wide Web consists of billions of pages linked to each other. These pages contain text, graphics, multimedia files, and other interactive software that are accessed using a browser. The World Wide Web was available to everyone on 23 August 1991.

When was the first search engine built?

In 1990! A 'web search engine' is a software system that is developed to search for information on the World Wide Web. The first search engine was called the Archie. It was created by Alan Emtage, Bill Heelan and J. Peter Deutsch, computer science students at McGill University in Montreal. Archie searched FTP sites to create an index of downloadable files.

Find out

What does CC mean in an email?

Pocket fact

Snail Mail!
A mail that is sent through the post office is now-a-days called 'snail mail'. This is because it is as slow as a snail as compared to email.

When was the first email sent?

In 1971! An email or electronic mail is a method of exchanging mails between people by electronic devices. Email was invented by an American computer programmer Ray Tomlinson. He implemented the first email program on the ARPANET and sent the first email to himself as a test message.

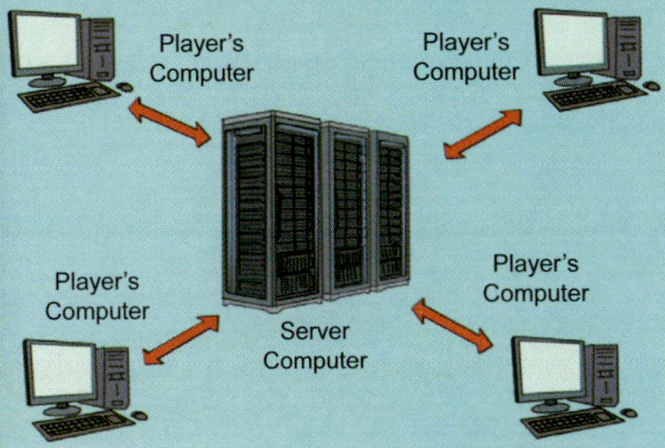

When is a computer called a server?

When it provides functionality to other programs or devices! A server is a computer program that is connected to other computers and manages network resources. It can provide different services such as control access to a network, send/receive e-mail, manage print jobs or host a website. Different computers can connect to a server through either a Local Area Network (LAN) or a Wide Area Network (WAN), such as the Internet.

Pocket fact

Mail Server!
A mail server is a remote or central computer that holds email messages for clients on a network. It is similar to a post office where mails are stored and sorted before sending them to the receiver.

Find out

How many digits are there in an IP address?

When does an address become an IP address?

When it is used to locate a computer! An IP (Internet Protocol) address is a number used to indicate the location of a computer or other device on a network. The IP address is just similar to your address, it allows data to reach the appropriate destination on a network and the Internet.

When do laptops overheat?

A laptop is said to be overheated when it generates more heat than it is designed to handle. Many times overheating is caused when a laptop's fan fails or is inadequate to cool it down. It can also occur due to poor ventilation, a bad cable, dust and dirt, an under-performing hard drive or an insufficient power supply.

Find out

What is a case fan?

Pocket fact

Revolutions per minute!
The speed of a computer or laptop fan is measured in revolutions per minute, or RPM. The higher the RPM rating, the faster the fan spins.

When does a laptop fan turn on?

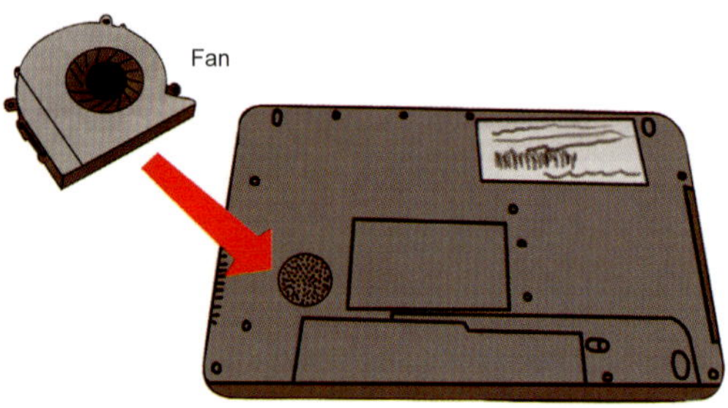

A computer or laptop fan is a hardware device that keeps it cool by circulating air to or from the laptop or a component. Laptop fan keeps running from the moment you turn on the Laptop. The fan sucks air from outside cools the device. Then, hot air is pushed out through the Fan Vent and the laptop is cooled.

When is a computer idle?

When its processor is not being used by any program! A program or task that runs on a computer system occupies a certain amount of processing time on the Central Processing Unit (CPU). When CPU has completed all its tasks and is not being used by any program, it is said to be idle.

Pocket fact

The Crescent Moon!
You may find the crescent moon symbol on a button on your computer case or a key. This symbol is used represent night time or, in other words, going to sleep.

Find out

How can you wake or get a computer out of sleep mode?

When does a computer sleep?

A computer doesn't sleep by itself but you can let it enter sleep mode when it is idle for a long time! It is a period of inactivity of the computer. The Sleep mode helps the computer conserve a lot of power while it is still on.

Index

http://www.

OTHER TITLES IN THIS SERIES